Coloring Book Japanese Anime Girl

By Weskerdcs

CONTENTS

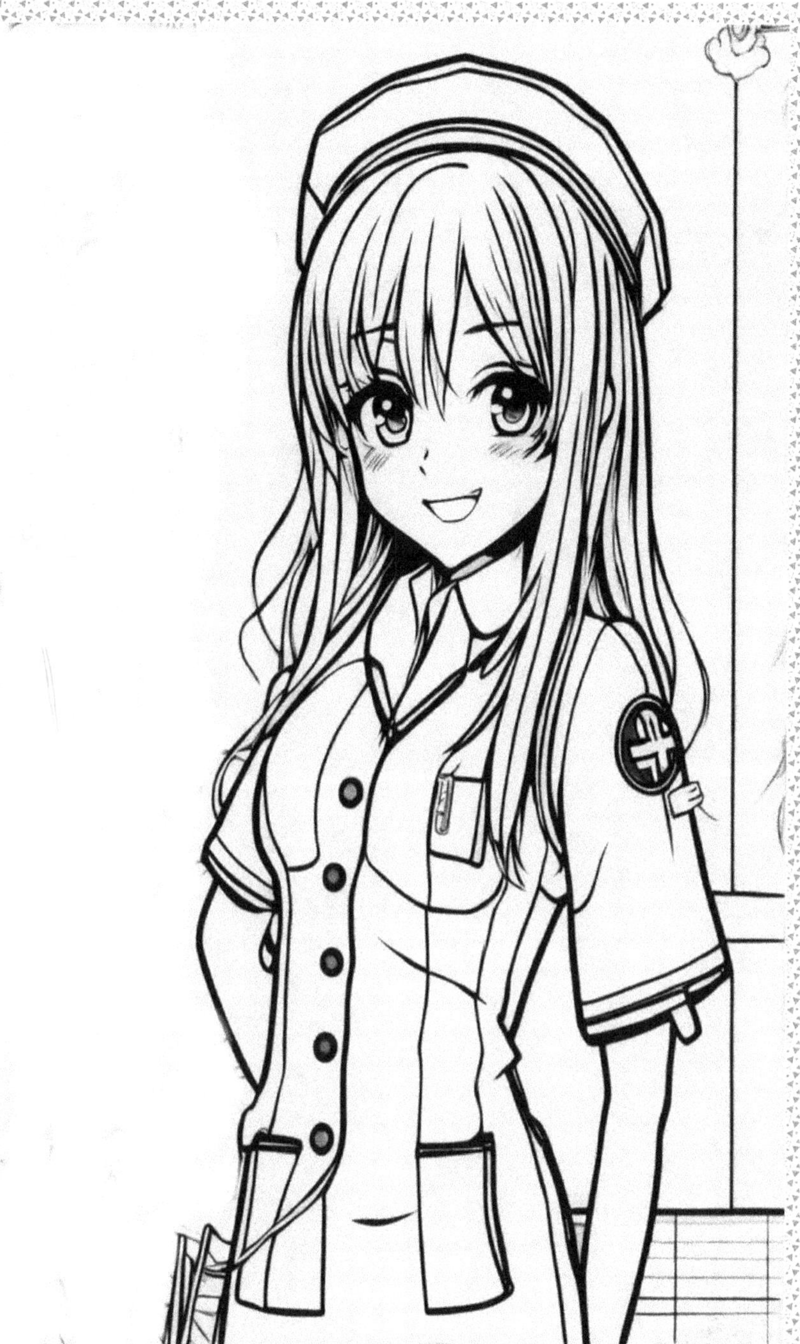

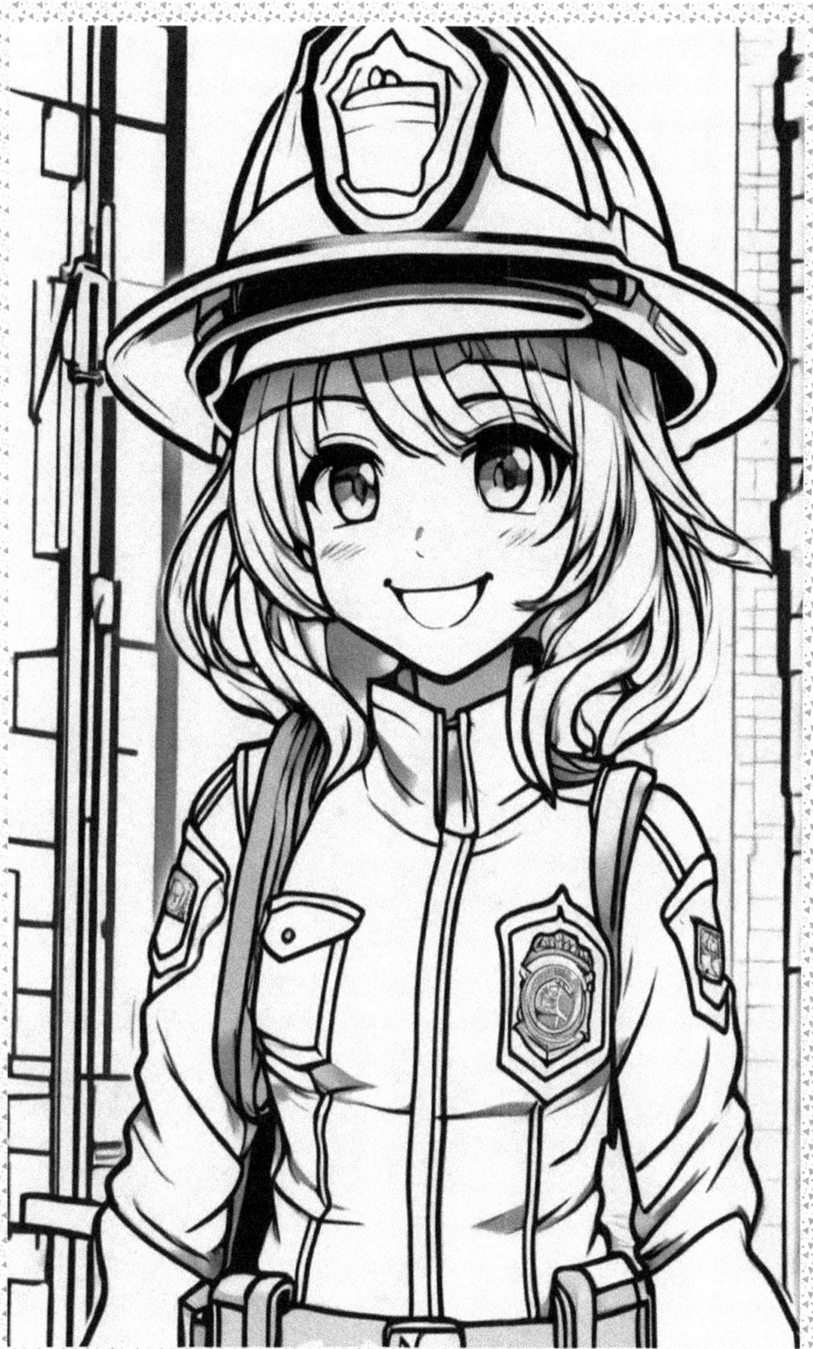

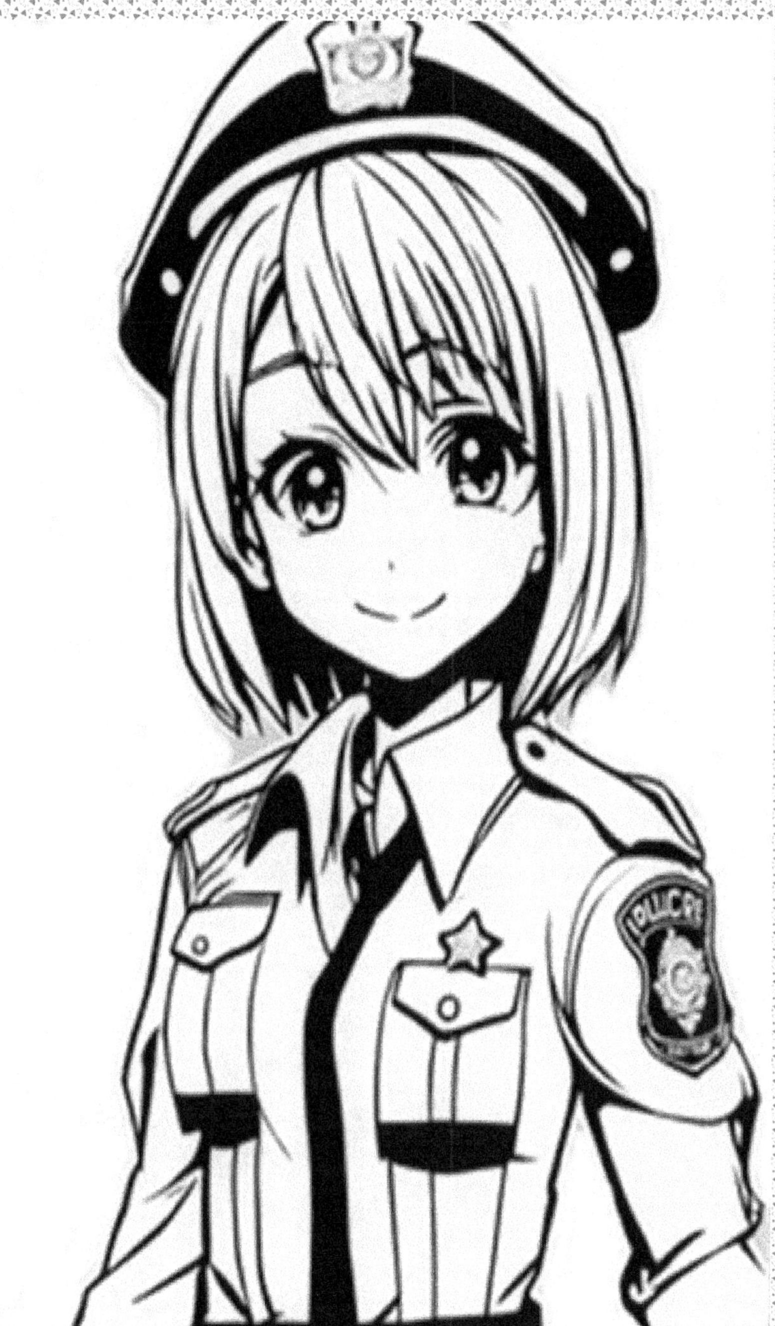

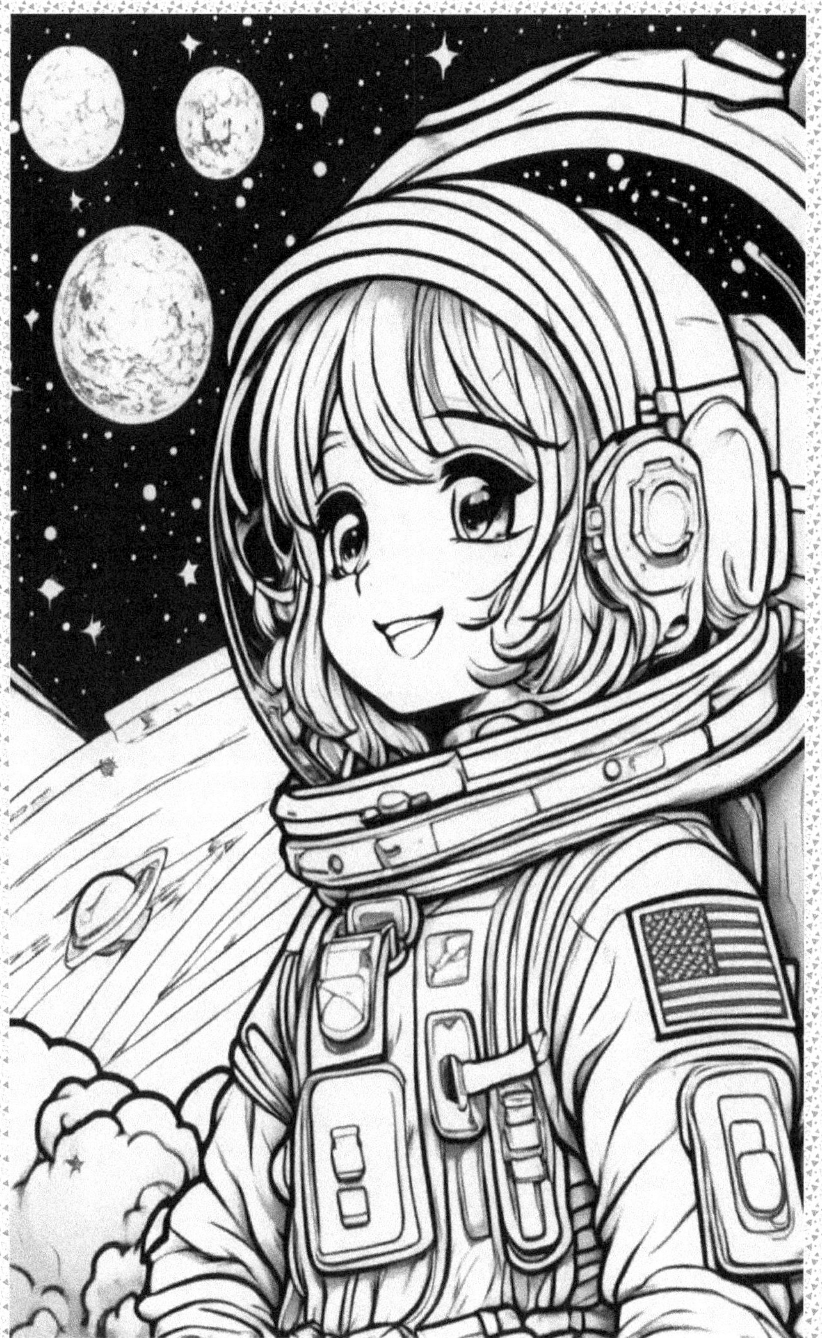

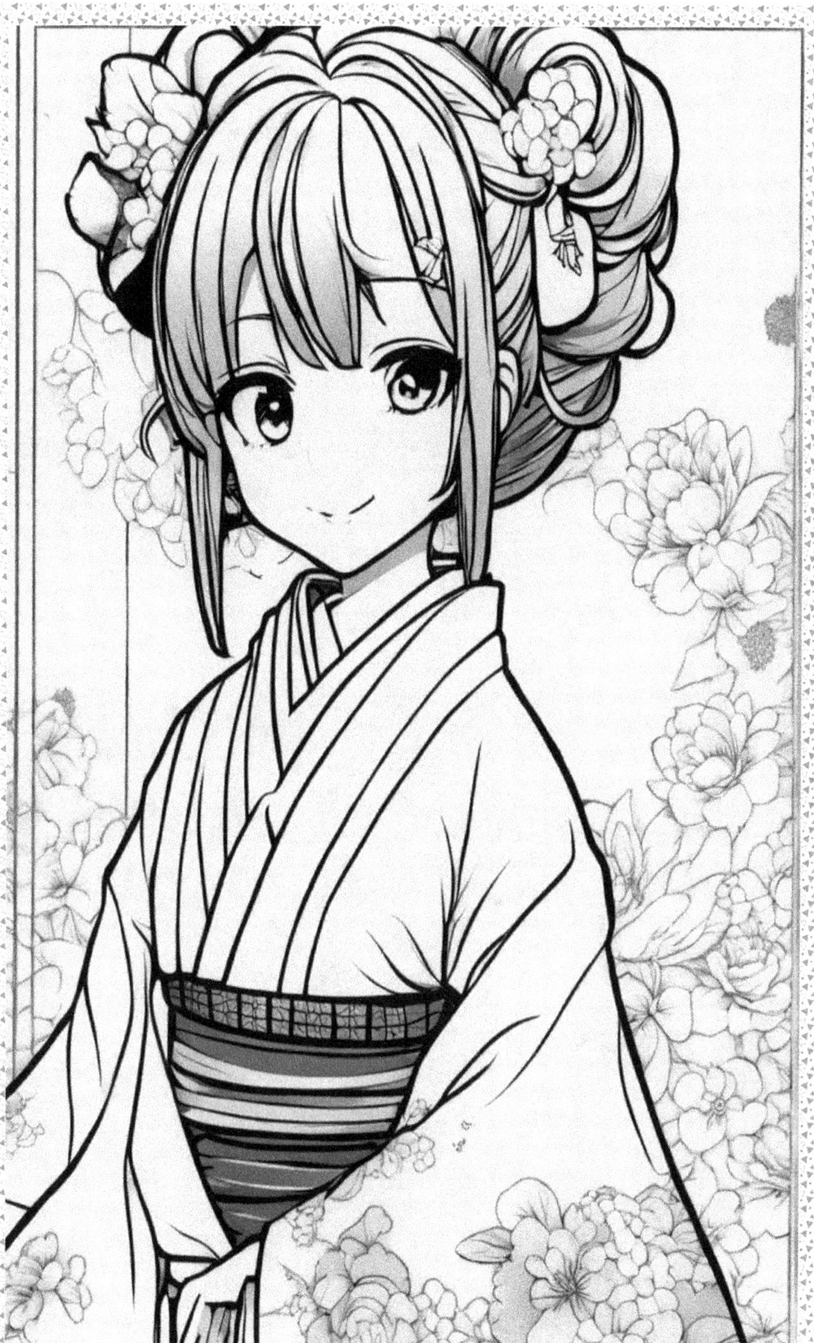

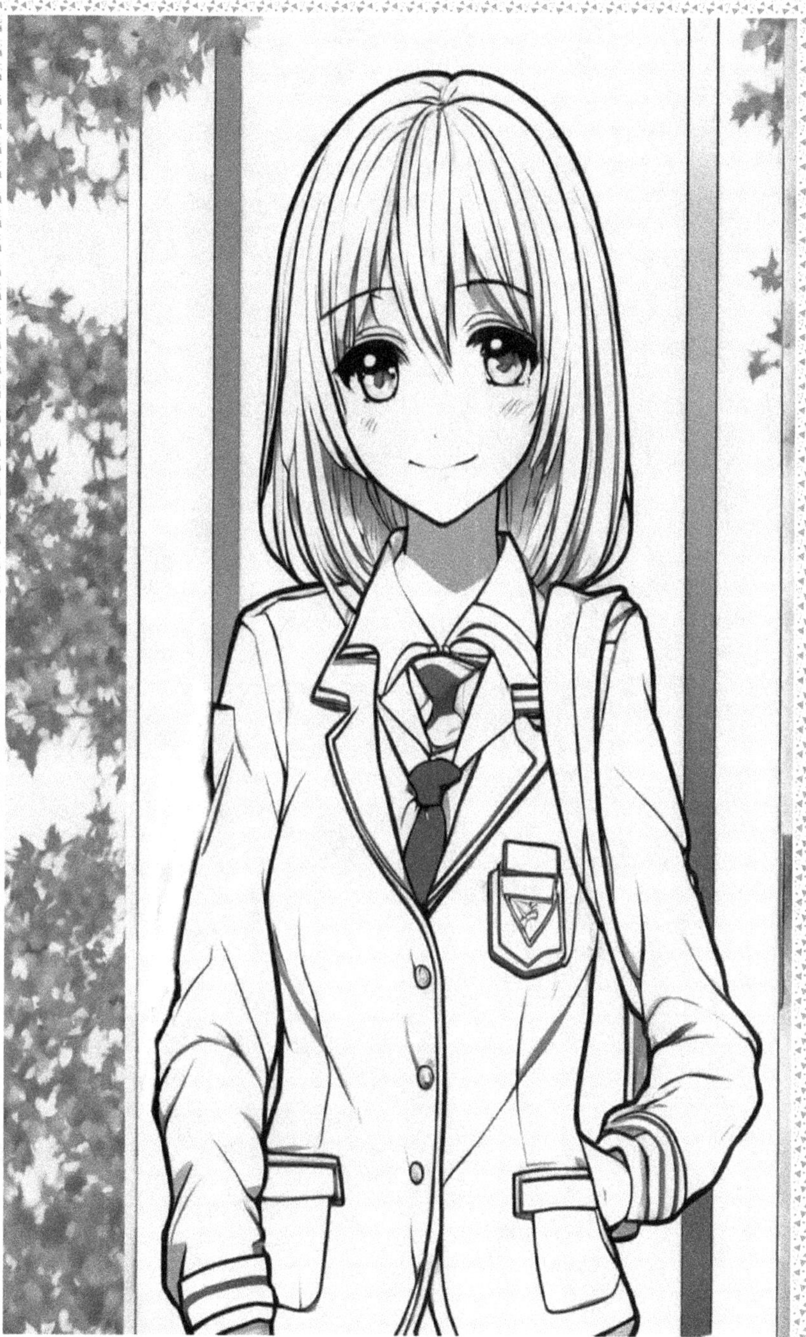

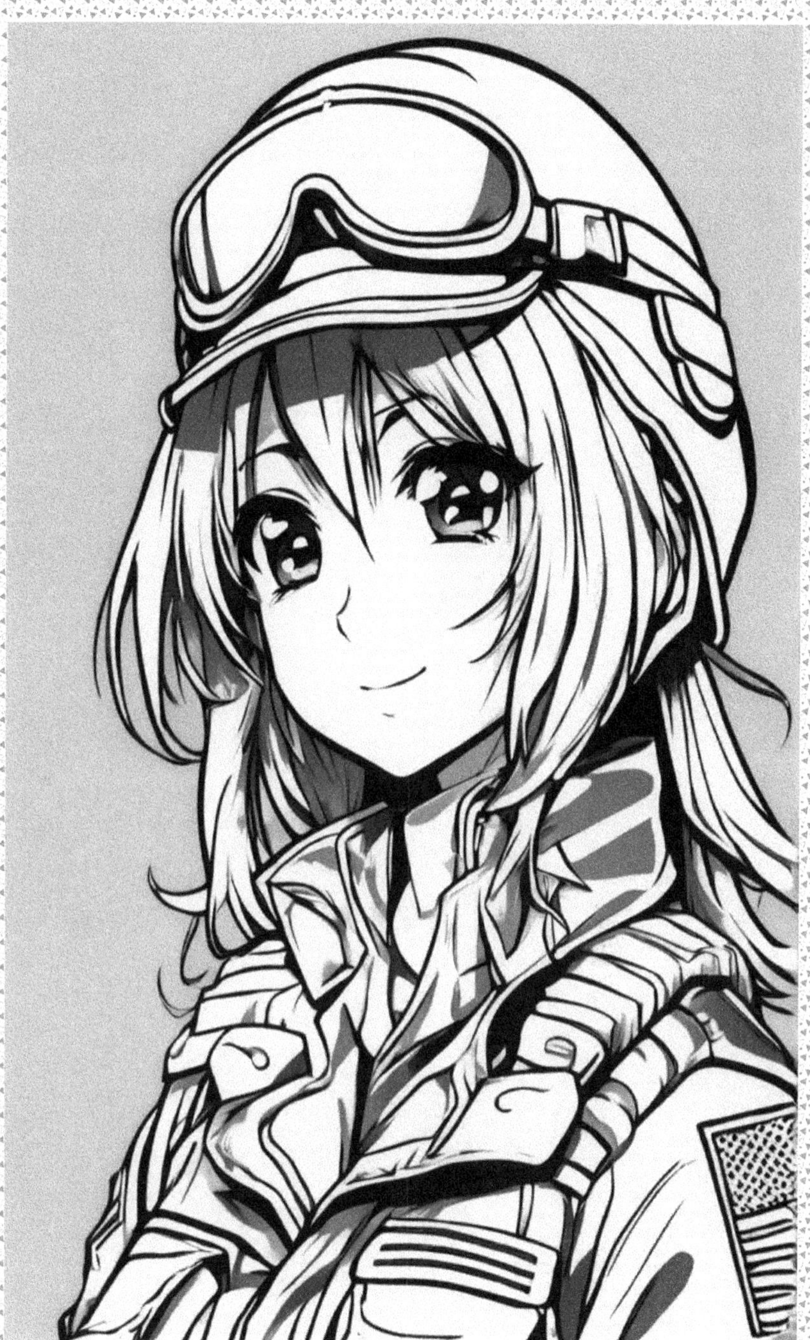

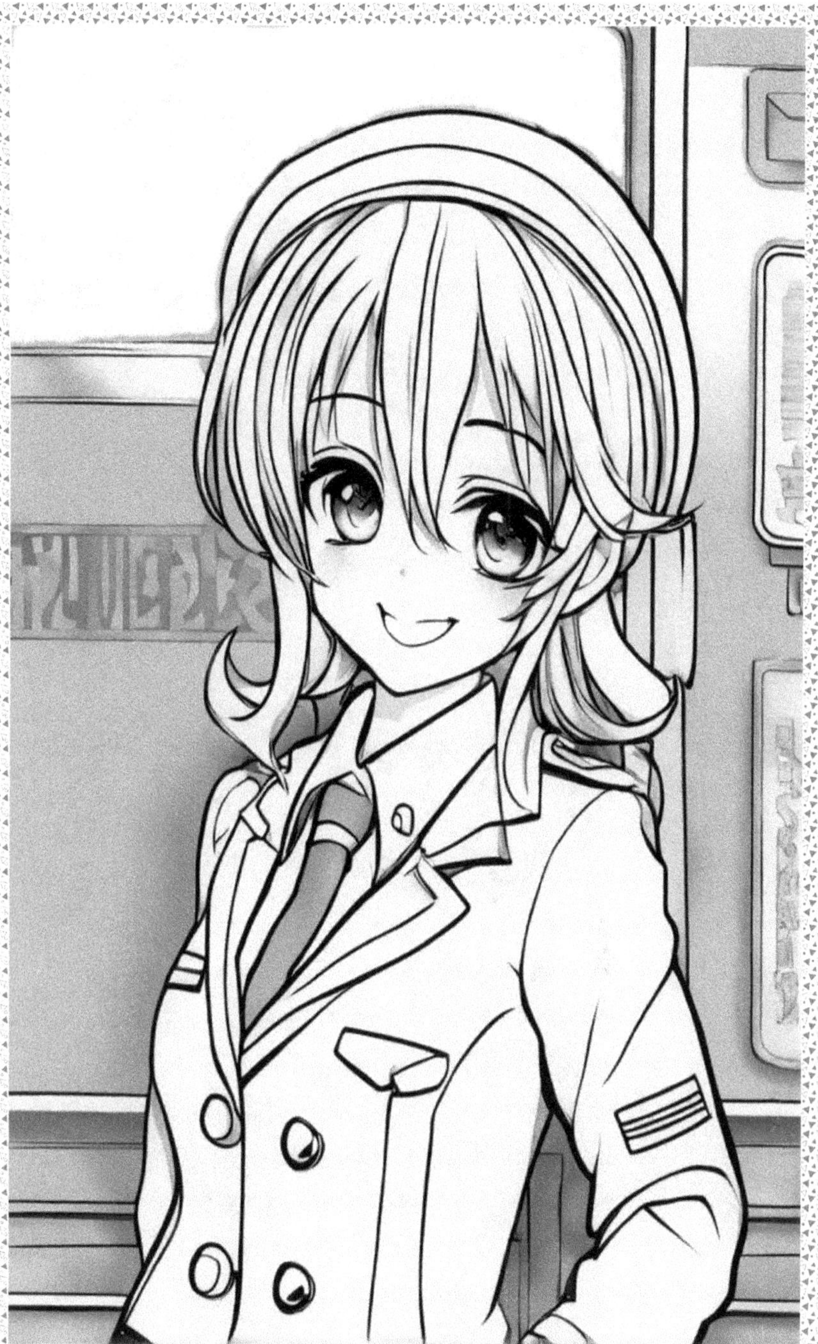

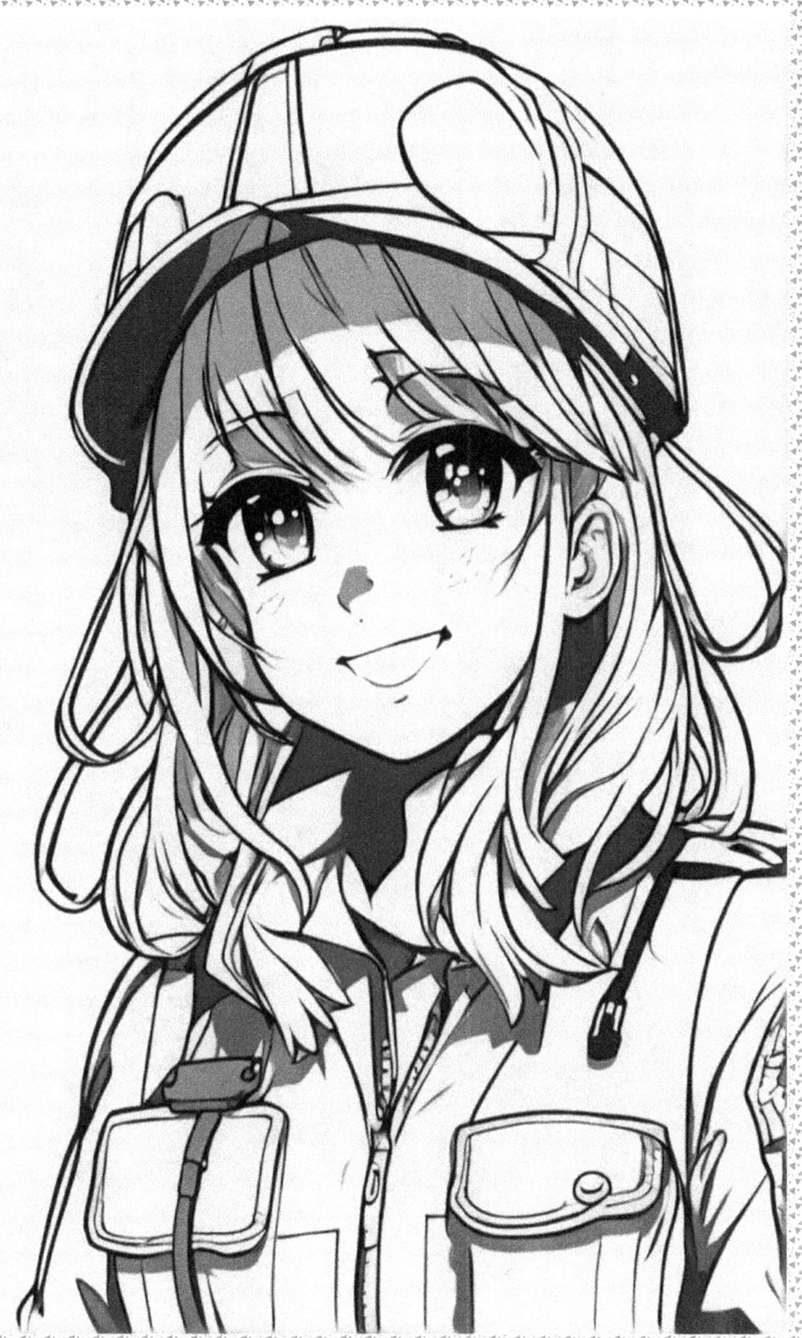

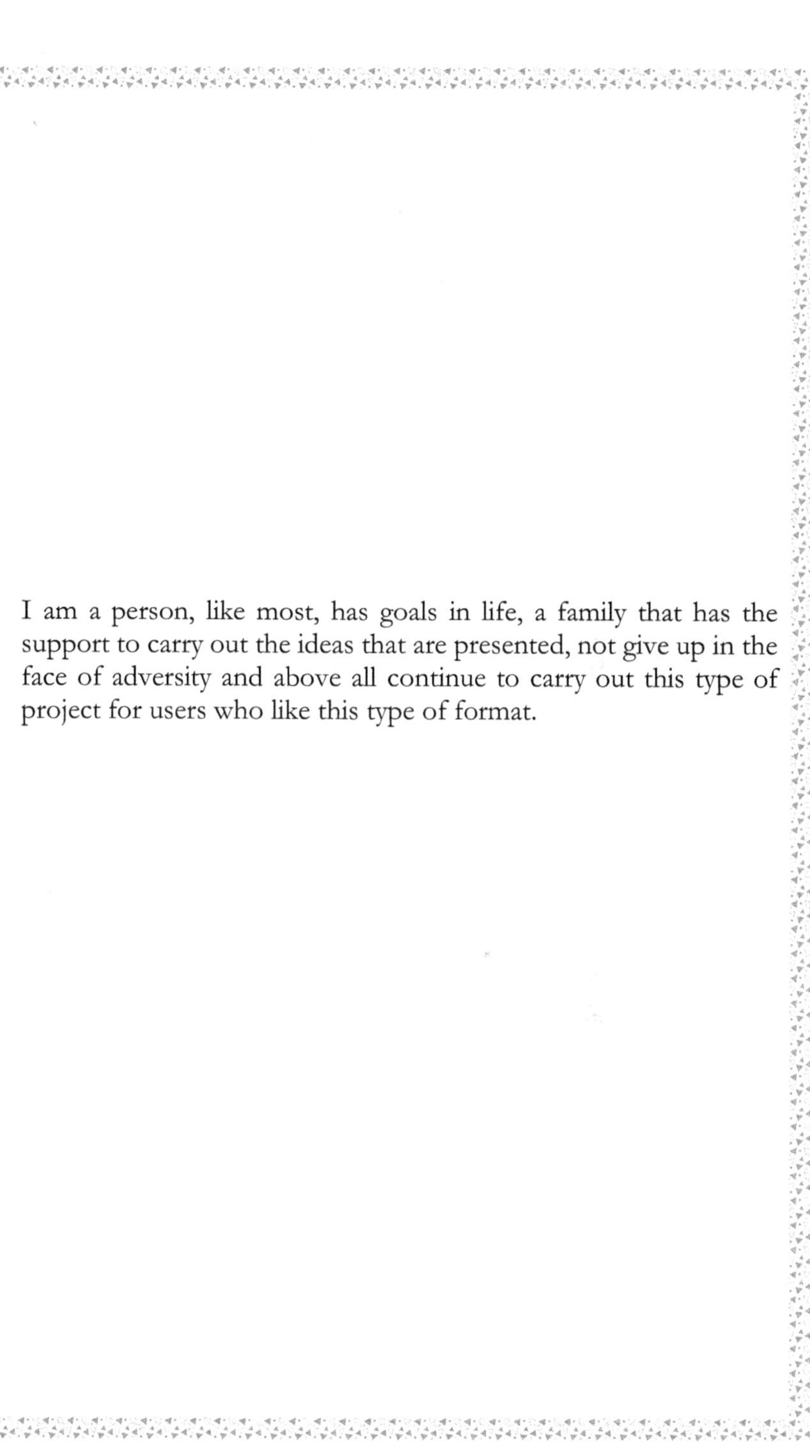

I am a person, like most, has goals in life, a family that has the support to carry out the ideas that are presented, not give up in the face of adversity and above all continue to carry out this type of project for users who like this type of format.